TAKE CARE
OF
YOURSELF

DEEPANSHI MUDGIL

Made with ♥ on the Notion Press Platform
www.notionpress.com

This book is Dedicated to my personal opinion about taking care of yourself.

Contents

ॐ श्री गणेशाय नमः

• vii •

Preface

Hello there,

If you picked this book, chances are you're like me- a 21 year old who is experiencing ups and down of life and bringing change for betterment in life by learning skills for taking care of self.

In this book i have shared my views that i established by my experience. This book isn't just for you but for me as well. it is a product of what i've learnt from my experiences. It is a product of my life lessons that i've learnt along the way. It is a guide that i wish i had when i was searching for direction in my life. This book is not lenghthy and will definetly not take much time to read. so, I hope you will enjoy my writing.

Acknowledgements

This book was purely written from the conclusion I got from my experiences. I would like to thank my parents who motivated me to pen down my thoughts. Your love and support mean everything to me. Thankyou for always believing in me.

My Ishwar who gave me the courage to write this book.

To all my friends and family whose words of wisdom and kindness lifted me up and motivated me to keep going.

And to the reader, thankyou for picking up this book. I hope that the words inside will help you on your journey of self-discovery.

With love and gratitude

(Deepanshi Mudgil)

ONE

INTRODUCTION

"To love oneself is the beginning of a lifelong romance."

-Oscar Wilde

Taking care of oneself is an art of making life simple and sorted. Your successful and dedicated efforts for yourself can take you to great heights. I don't know how many of you have heard...but there is a very catchy line from a popular prayer – "dusro say Pehle khud ki jay karein" which means that you have to prioritize yourself first.

Taking care of yourself is your responsibility. No one else is responsible for you... it's just you! You have the key to making yourself happy, establishing an alluring impact of your personality. If you give that key to anyone than you may lose the lock at any time because it can be misused at any time. You may feel that the person you are trusting is genuine but always remember that the person you are trusting can change his colour at any time. Therefore, be prepared to be cheated.

You have the ability to handle yourself it's just that you don't recognize your strength and they remain hidden. To know yourself you have to make an effort yourself, no one else will come to make this effort.

Just imagine that you live with such a person that all your emotions depend on him, if he keeps you happy then you become happy and someday if he does not talk to you nicely then you become sad, so do you think that this is right?

Make yourself so capable that you are not dependent on anyone and your personality becomes more attractive and composed.

TWO

BE THE CONTROLLER OF YOUR ACTIONS

Your actions reflect your personality. Your image is what you do and portray. The way you resolve conflict of your thoughts and perform actions depends upon the nourishment of an individual. A person's nourishment is done by the people around him in childhood, such as his parents and teachers, but when he grows up, he nourishes himself and gives a way to his thoughts. A person gets his thoughts in the right direction by reading right books, being with people who will help steer you in the right direction. Your actions must be constructive. It must make you a better person. One cannot deny that actions are often wrecked with emotions and feelings. when power of thinking and acting is dominated by emotions and feelings, even the best in you can be vanished and ultimately you loose control over yourself. The ultimate solution to get control over your actions is continuous efforts on yourself. Your hard work on yourself can never go in vain, only your efforts will lead you to success. Have you ever seen a confused person taking right decision for his actions? It is very important to have clear intellect to perform right actions. You are responsible for every action you do, so whatever you do, try to do it thoughtfully. It's not that no one can ever make mistake, after all we all are humans and mistakes will happen, but learning from each mistake and moving on is a wise decision. The mistakes you have made should not have a negative impact on your present, rather it should lead you towards betterment.

HACKS TO CONTROL ONE'S ACTIONS

PLAN BEFORE ACTING: Before doing anything, you should carefully evaluate its effects and only then take any step. Be prepared for the consequence of whatever action you are taking.

MANAGEMENT OF EMOTIONS: An essential component of taking right action involves only you- knowing your own emotions is very important and more important is how you will control them. Classify your emotions and work on them. Evaluate your emotions before taking any step. Tranquility helps you a lot in managing your emotions.

UNDERSTANDING THE SITUATION: Before taking any action, you must evaluate your situation because whatever action you take should be according to your situation. You should learn the art of moulding yourself with every changing situation.

QUIT BLAMING OTHERS: It is wrong to blame others for your actions. You yourself is responsible for every action you do. You should have control over each action you perform. If you once understand that you are responsible for your actions, then you will think wisely before doing anything because ultimately its result will affect you only.

FOLOWING AN ACTIVE ROUTINE: Your laziness is your biggest enemy, so try to make your routine active. Here active routine means that whatever work you are doing, you are giving hundred percent dedication. There should be no room for laziness in your life. You should do every task of your day with passion and try to put your best into that thing.

CLARITY OF THOUGHTS: It is very important to have clarity of thoughts in your life. If you are able to think clearly, then you will be able to take actions clearly too. Confused state of mind can impact actions negatively therefore always be clear with your thoughts.

THREE
LEARNING FROM MISTAKES

"Do not fear mistakes. You will know failure. Continue to reach out."

-Benjamin Franklin

A person should always learn from his mistakes. Making mistakes is not a sin but repeating them is stupidity. You must always take lessons from your mistakes and keep moving forward with new and leveled up spirit. Don't let your mistakes overpower and influence you negatively. Mistakes work as a tool to improve self of an individual. Yes, but this doesn't mean that you will keep making mistakes. You should not commit any mistake intentionally. One must be conscious about his actions because it reduces the chances of you making mistakes. You should always remember that your responsibility is your own and not anyone else's, it's just you who is responsible for each and every action that you do.

MEASURES TO LEARN FROM YOUR MISTAKES

ACKNOWLEDGING YOUR ERRORS: It is a big deal to accept your mistakes. Not everyone has a mindset of accepting the mistakes that one does. If you do not accept your mistakes then how will you move forward. So always acknowledge the mistakes done by you and keep the spirit of moving further.

ACCEPT RESPONSIBILITY: You should accept that you are responsible for your every action and not anyone else. So never blame anyone for your act. Circumstances of an individual can make him feel that he is not responsible for his act but always remember that at the end it is always you who act or react to circumstances. It's upon you what you choose to do.

EVALUATING ACTIONS: Evaluate your actions. Brainstorm future impact of your act. Categorize your actions in right and wrong on the basis of its effect.

SEEKING FEEDBACK: In case if you are unable to understand what your mistake is or how you can improve further, then you can take suggestions from trusted people around you like your parents, teacher, friend etc.

ANALYZING SITUATION: Always analyse your situation, see how you are behaving in a particular situation and improve wherever you feel you need to improve.

PROMPTING QUESTIONS TO YOURSELF: Try to ask questions to yourself. for every action that you do always try to put a question for your act and ask yourself about the solution for improving further.

FOUR

BE THE CONTROLLER OF YOUR EMOTION

"Emotions can be the enemy, if you give into your emotions, you lose yourself. you must be at one with your emotions, because the body always follows the mind".

-Bruce Lee

Emotions can work for you in both good and bad way, it depends on how you utilize your emotions. It is your responsibility to control your emotions. Keeping your emotions under control is not a one-day job rather it may take a long time and your unparallel efforts. Keeping your emotions under control is not as easy as it sounds, sometimes it becomes very difficult. Your emotions are not a switch that when you feel like it, you become happy, sad. No, it can take lot of time and energy to keep your emotions under your control and for this, take as much time as you require, but always keep patience. You are a human being, you will get angry, frustrated, feel pain, you will feel every emotion that human being feels and I will not ask you to supress them rather I'll suggest to manage them. Supposethere is a person who gets very angry, then instead of shouting and repeatedly showing his anger to the people around him, he should release his anger and energy in some other place. He should channel his energy towards something which at the end benefit him and bring positive outcome. You may have to face mental conflict to control your emotions but trust me, once you learn to control your emotions, this mental conflict will last only for a few days, after which you will find balance in yourself.

KEY STRATEGIES TO CONTROL EMOTIONS

LABELING EMOTIONS:The most important thing in controlling your emotions is labelling them. Try to know about what kind of emotions you are dealing with, what is causing the turmoil inside you because if you yourself don't know about your emotions then how will you manage them? Supposing you are very sensitive, then you will try to find the solution accordingly. So always label your emotions so that you can find solution for yourself and work towards its management.

CALMING ONESELF:Try to calm yourself by taking deep breath and doing breathing exercise by doing this one can calm body's physiological response to stress and intense emotions.

HEALTHY EATING HABITS:Healthy eating is very important to control your emotions because by adopting healthy eating habits your body will make good cells and will release good hormones which will ultimately be very helpful for managing your emotions.

SEEKING PROFESSIONAL HELP:If you think that you need someone to help controlling your emotions then don't hesitate to seek professional help. Step out and take support so that you manage your emotions well.

MINDFULNESS:Pay attention to your feelings and thoughts without judging yourself. observe your emotions, what kind of emotions you face in different situations and try to find its solution by brainstorming the scenario.

EXPRESS YOUSELF:It is very important to express your emotions. If you feel like crying, then cry but do not supress your emotions. Yes, I am not saying to express your emotions in front of everyone rather express it to someone who you feel is genuine and trustworthy. If you can not rely on anyone then express your emotions to yourself by standing in front of mirror or just by having conversation with yourself.

FIVE

CLARITY OF VISION

> *"Clarity of vision creates clarity of priorities"*
>
> -John C. Maxwell

Clarity of vision means having a clear, systematic and well-planned roadmap of your actions. It means to know what exactly you want in your life. Your life is a beautiful journey of your own. It's you who decide your actions to achieve clear understanding of your goal. Clear vision leads to clarity of thoughts and all this together results in clear and productive actions which bring desired outcomes.

For having clarity of vision firstly you have to do SELF ASSESSMENT, in which you have to understand about your strengths, passion, interest, weak point, attitude and your aptitude. This will help you to understand yourself.

Then, set up your goals as this will provide direction in your life. Goal setting eradicates vagueness, obscurity and clouded perspective from life which results in clear path for life.

After goal setting develop an action plan, develop strategies to reach the desired goal. These strategies will help you to identify potential obstacles and provide you a clear roadmap for your actions.

In order to reach the goal, you have to act according to your vision and have to regular review the progress made by you and make adjustments as per the need.

SIX

ART OF COMMUNICATION

"Communication is your ticket to success if you pay attention and learn to do it effectively"

-Theo Gold

The art of communication involves the transmission of your thoughts in proficient and operative way. While communicating you have to be very mindful. Communication is not always between you and the other person it is with yourself too. While communicating with yourself you have to be understand that you have to be very conscious about the sentences you deliver to yourself. There is a vacuum inside us and it should be tackled with due care.

<u>KEY ASPECTS OF SELF COMMUNICATION</u>

ASK QUESTIONS TO YOURSELF to explore your thoughts and emotions. This will help you to label your actions and the reason behind them.

POSITIVE TALK WITH THE SELF is very important to motivate the self. Replace your negative self-talk with affirmative sentences and encourage yourself to participate actively in every aspect.

PEN DOWN YOUR EMOTIONS as this will help you to gain clarity about yourself.

BE HONEST WITH THE SELF, don't feel ashamed of examining challenging thoughts and emotions.

AVOID SELF CRITICISM, Treat yourself with same compassion you would extend to a friend. "Be kind to yourself"

While communicating with others one must be very confident about his speech, body language and eye contact. With good communication skills, you can get even the toughest tasks done easily. Whenever you are talking to a person, you should make sure that your body language is correct, you are making eye contact with the other person, your facial expressions should be simple and whatever you are saying should make sense. Be an active listener, don't hurry while keeping your point in front of the person. Try to understand other point of view and analyse the context.

Be present in the moment, stay focused and avoid distractions. Even if you do not agree with someone's view you should still try to talk to them in an affirmative manner. In this way you will be able to convince the person. Your communication should not turn into a fight or an argument and for this, whatever point of view you are keeping, present it in right tone. If you want the other person to be convinced by you then try to be confident while speaking, try healthy communication in which you must respect the other person's view.

KEY POINTS TO IMPROVE COMMUNICATION SKILLS:

Practice in front of mirror.

Be confident.

Avoid vagueness while speaking.

Make proper eye contact

Engage facts while talking

Keep your tone soft

Respect the person to whom you are communicating

Be an active listener

SEVEN

HAPPINESS IS THE KEY FOR LEADING A SMOOTH LIFE

"It isn't what you have or who you are or where you are or what you are doing that makes you happy or unhappy. It is what you think about it." -Dale Carnegie

Responsibility of your happiness is yours because you cannot depend on anyone else for your happiness. If you give the key of your happiness to someone else, then you become dependent on the other person and that person can make you act according to his wishes.

So, always keep the key of your happiness with yourself.

People living around you can be a source of your happiness but they cannot be owner. It is your responsibility to find source of happiness all the time.

Even if you are feeling down, you should always try to bring enthusiasm in yourself. suppose, if you are sad and you are still listening to sad songs, then it means that you are promoting sadness. Instead of this, you should try to distract your mind and find happiness even in the smallest thing.

It may not be possible to remain happy and excited all the time, but there is nothing wrong in making effort to lift up your mood.

HACKS TO REMAIN HAPPY:

Eat well.

Exercise

Listening to cheerful music.

Dancing the way, you want.

Express gratitude.

Breathing exercise.

Spend time in nature.

Practice self-care.

Take proper sleep.

Follow a routine.

Distract your mind.

Keep yourself busy.

Follow your passion.

Meditate.

Spend time with loved ones.

Travel to your favourite places.

Express your feelings.